Ask AI

ROBBERT VAN EMPEL

ASK AI

Prompting Made Simple
Go from Beginner to Pro

Publisher The Future

For any copies of this book
please contact
info@thefuture.im

Design and layout: The Future, Haarlem
Graphic production: The Future, Haarlem

ISBN 978 9 08357 591 9
NUR 600
Keywords AI, artificial intelligence,
prompting, work efficiency,
work improvement

www.thefuture.im

For Pelle. In a world full of answers, it is the art of asking that guides us toward tomorrow.

Contents

Introduction

You hear it everywhere: on the news, at work, maybe even at the kitchen table. The term "AI" has become inescapable. It sounds big, smart, and maybe a little intimidating. Like it's something reserved for scientists in white lab coats or computer nerds who spend all day tinkering with code.

But what if I told you that AI is really just a new kind of tool? A tool that anyone can learn to use. Just like you learned to ride a bike or figured out how to use a smartphone. It might take some getting used to at first, but pretty soon, you won't be able to imagine life without it.

This book is your guide to that new tool. I wrote it because I believe that talking to an AI should be as easy as talking to a person. That's why I've left out all the difficult and technical terms. Instead, using simple language and clear examples, I'll show you how you can be the one in charge of AI.

You'll discover how to ask the right questions to get the exact answers you're looking for. Whether you need help writing an email, are searching for a creative idea for your job, or are simply curious about what's possible.

Think of this book as your first step into a new world. A world where you're not just talking about the future, but are actively helping to build it. Are you ready? Let's start this adventure together.

1. The World of AI

"Innovation distinguishes between a leader and a follower" - *Steve Jobs*

This one sentence says it all: if you want to get ahead, you have to innovate. And that means you need to be able to talk to AI. That's why I wrote this book, because I believe that anyone–yes, truly anyone–can learn how to do this.

Of course, you've heard of artificial intelligence before, or as many people call it now, AI. But what we're actually talking about is a specific type of AI: Large Language Models, or LLMs. Imagine a computer that has read an incredible number of books, articles, and websites–so many that it understands human language extremely well and can even write new text itself. That's basically what an LLM is. For the sake of simplicity, I'll stick to the word AI in this book, but just know that when I do, I'm actually referring to an LLM.

Now, you might be thinking, "Wow, that sounds complicated!" And to be fair, most books and explanations you find on this topic are full of technical jargon. This often makes people feel insecure or think it's not for them. But it doesn't have to be that way at all. My mission with this book is to explain all that complicated stuff in a super simple way, so that you can understand it, even as a beginner.

Think of it like learning to talk to a new friend. It might be a little awkward at first, but once you get to know them better, you can have the best conversations and do the coolest things. The commands and questions you give to an AI are called "prompts." And that's what this entire book is about: how you can become a master at crafting those prompts.

What Are Prompts and Why Are They So Important?

Okay, so what exactly is a "prompt"? A prompt is basically just an instruction, a question, or a starting sentence that you give to an AI. Compare it to making a wish to a genie in a magic lamp. If you just mumble, "I want something nice," the genie won't really know what to give you. But if you say, "Genie, I wish for a beautiful, red sports car with a seven-speed transmission," you're much more likely to get what you want.

It works the same way with AI. The clearer and more specific your prompt is, the better the AI will understand you, and the better the answer you'll get back will be. And the great thing is, anyone can write a prompt. You don't have to be a computer nerd or a scientist to do it.

Why is this so important? These AIs are a kind of prediction machine. When you start a sentence, the AI tries to predict which word will best fit next, based on everything it has learned. Your prompt is the start of that sentence. If your starting point is unclear or messy, the AI's prediction will also be messy, and you might get a useless answer.

So, a good prompt is the key to having a good conversation with AI. It ensures that you are in control and that the AI does what you want, not the other way around.

The RAFT Method

When I first started exploring prompts, I found it was sometimes pretty hard to figure out where to begin. That's why I developed a simple tool for myself, which I call the **RAFT method**. The name works as a great metaphor: it's the best foundational method to build a raft that helps you navigate the sea of AI. RAFT is an acronym that stands for:

- **R**ole: What role or persona should the AI adopt? Should it answer as an expert in space travel? As a funny pirate? As a helpful customer service representative? Or maybe as an objective journalist?
- **A**udience: Who is the answer intended for? Are you writing something for an 8-year-old child? For your boss? For a friend who knows nothing about the topic? Or for experts who want a lot of detail?

- **F**ormat: How do you want to receive the AI's answer? Do you want a story in continuous prose? A bulleted list? A table with rows and columns? Maybe even computer code?
- **T**ask: What exactly do you want the AI to do for you? What is the specific goal or end result you want to achieve? Do you want a summary of a long text? To write a poem? An answer to a tough question? A list of ideas?

Let's take a simple example. Imagine you want to create a short story for your nephew. Using the RAFT method, you might think:

- **R**ole: The AI should write like an old, wise wizard.
- **A**udience: It's for my 8-year-old nephew.
- **F**ormat: The story should be about three paragraphs long.
- **T**ask: A short, exciting story.

Your prompt could then be: "Act as an old, wise wizard (**Role**) and write for an 8-year-old child (**Audience**). The output should be a short, exciting story (**Task**) of about three paragraphs (**Format**) about a boy who meets a talking squirrel."

In Table 1, you can see the RAFT method explained clearly once again.

The RAFT method is a good start. It helps you think in a structured way about what to put in your prompt. It ensures you don't forget the most important ingredients. But–and this is very important–RAFT is for beginner prompts. It's a great way to get started, but it's not enough to become a true prompt expert. There are many more smart tricks and techniques you can learn to get even better answers.

Element	Explanation	Example
Role	What role or persona should the AI adopt?	"Act as an expert...", "Answer as a travel guide...", "You are a poet..."
Audience	Who is the answer intended for?	"...for a beginner", "...for my manager", "...in language a child can understand"
Format	How do you want to receive the AI's answer?	"...in a list", "...in a maximum of 100 words", "...as a table"
Task	What exactly do you want the AI to do for you?	"Write a poem...", "Summarize this text...", "Give 5 ideas for..."

Table 1: The RAFT method.

RAFT

What is Prompt Engineering?

Now that we know what a prompt is, and we even have an initial method (RAFT) to think about it, we can talk about "prompt engineering." That might sound very technical again, but it's really not that bad. Prompt engineering is the art of designing and refining those prompts. It's the process of tinkering, puzzling, and experimenting with your questions to the AI until you get exactly the answer you're looking for, in the precise way you want it.

Imagine you're a detective trying to solve a mystery. You ask questions, you try different angles, you pay attention to small details. That's a bit like what a prompt engineer does. You try different words, you change the order of the sentences, you add extra information or take things away. You are constantly "tinkering" to create the very best prompt for your specific goal.

It's a process of trial and error. Sometimes your first idea for a prompt works perfectly right away, and you get exactly the answer you want, but it's more likely that you'll need a few tries. That's perfectly okay; it's just part of the process. So, prompt engineering isn't just about typing a question and getting an answer from an AI. It's a skill that you can develop. It's about understanding how these smart AIs think and how you can best guide them.

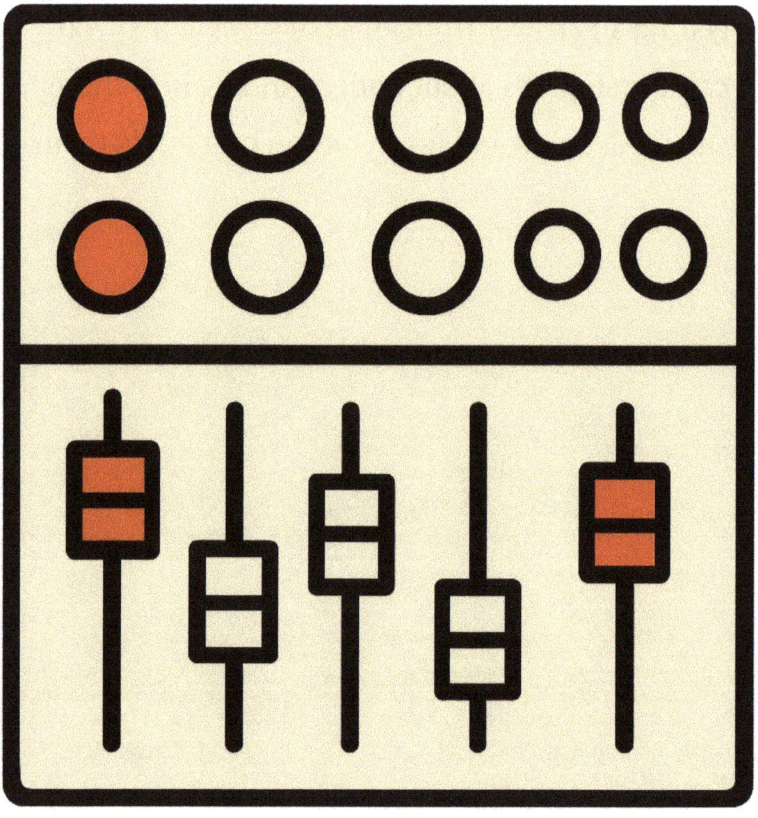

2. Turning the Dials

When you talk to an AI, the prompt is obviously super important. But did you know there are also a kind of "settings" or "dials" you can play with? This is especially true when you're not just using a standard chatbot, but working directly with AI models through special programs or platforms. Think of a radio. You don't just choose which song you want to hear (that's your prompt), but you can also turn the volume knob or adjust the bass and treble. Those knobs on the radio change how the song sounds. The settings of an AI work a bit like that. They change how the AI responds to your prompt. Let's take a look at a few of those "dials."

How long should the response be?

One of the first dials you'll often encounter is the "response length" (output length). With this, you can tell the AI roughly how much text it's allowed to generate. This usually isn't measured in words or sentences, but in something called "tokens."

What are tokens? Tokens are the basic building blocks of language as an AI sees them. you can compare them to Lego bricks. A whole word can be one token (like "dog"), but sometimes a part of a word (like "in-cred-i-ble") is split into multiple tokens. Even punctuation marks like a period or a comma can be their own token. So, if you ask the AI for a response of 50 tokens, you mean 50 of those "Lego bricks" of text.

Why is this important? If you set the output length too short, say only 10 tokens, the AI might stop mid-sentence before it has made its point. That's obviously not very useful. But if you set the length too long, the AI might start rambling on and give you much more information than you need. Furthermore, the more tokens the AI generates, the more computing power it costs. And more computing power often means it consumes more "energy" and can ultimately cost more money, especially if you're using AI for business purposes. So, we want just enough tokens for a good and complete answer, without any waste.

It's also good to know that simply shortening the output length doesn't make the AI use shorter sentences. It just stops predicting new tokens when the limit is reached. So, if you want a short answer, you often need to make that clear in your prompt itself, in addition to setting the token limit.

Letting the AI Guess a Little

AIs don't just randomly pick the next word when they generate a response. They look at all the words they know and calculate a kind of score for each one: how likely is it that this word comes next, given the prompt and what has already been said? A choice is then made from those words.

These "sampling controls" are the dials we can use to influence how the AI makes that choice from the words with different scores. It's as if we're letting the AI "guess" a little, but we get to set the rules for that guessing game. The three most important dials for this are temperature, Top-K, and Top-P.

The Temperature Dial

The "temperature dial" is a very interesting one. This setting determines how "predictable" or how "creative" (or "random") the AI is when choosing the next word.

- **Low temperature** (e.g., 0 or a number close to 0, like 0.2): When you set the temperature low, the AI becomes very well-behaved and cautious. It will almost always choose the word with the absolute highest score–the most logical and predictable word. This is very useful when you want a factual answer, or when there is only one correct answer possible. Think of a math problem or translating a word. You don't want any surprises. A temperature of 0 means the AI will always pick the most likely word (though there can still be some randomness if scores are tied).
- **High temperature** (e.g., 1, or even higher like 1.5): If you turn the temperature up, the AI becomes more adventurous and dares to gamble more. It won't necessarily choose the most logical word, but might also pick words that are slightly less probable. This can lead to very creative and original answers. This is great if you want the AI to write a story or brainstorm new ideas. The

downside is that the answers can sometimes be a bit strange, incoherent, or even complete nonsense, precisely because the AI is taking more risks.

You can compare it to an ice cream shop. Imagine there are many different flavors. At a low temperature, you always choose vanilla because it's safe and predictable. At a high temperature, you might dare to try "peanut butter and pickle ice cream"–it could be surprisingly delicious, or it could be disgusting.

So, there is no "best" temperature; it depends entirely on what you want to achieve with your prompt (in other words, the Task from the RAFT method). For a business summary, you want a low temperature, but for coming up with a fantasy story, you might want a high one. It's a strategic choice, and it's fun to experiment with it to see what effect it has.

Top-K and Top-P

Besides temperature, there are two other dials that help determine how the AI chooses its next words: Top-K and Top-P (Top-P is also called "nucleus sampling"). These settings help to limit the AI's choices a bit, so it doesn't have to choose from too many words, which can improve the quality of the responses.

- **Top-K**: Imagine that after calculating a score for all possible next words, the AI creates a ranked list of the most likely words. With Top-K, you tell the AI: "Only look at the top K words on that list and choose the next word from that group." The "K" is a number you set yourself. For example, if you set K to 5, the AI only considers the 5 most likely words and ignores the rest. If you set K to 1, the AI always chooses the very top word on the list (which is the same as "greedy decoding," the most "stingy" or cautious choice). A higher K provides more variety, while a lower K makes it more predictable. A simple example: The AI has to choose the next word after "The cat climbed into the...". The top 5 most likely words might be: 1. tree (score 0.5), 2. pole (score 0.2), 3. curtains (score 0.1), 4. car (score 0.05), 5. sky (score 0.02). If Top-K is set to 3, the AI will only choose from "tree," "pole," or "curtains."

- **Top-P** (nucleus sampling): This dial works a little differently. Instead of choosing a fixed number of words (like with Top-K), here you look at the cumulative scores of the words. You set a threshold "P," for example, 0.9 (which means 90%). The AI then starts at the top of the ranked list of most likely words and adds their scores together until the sum reaches or exceeds the threshold "P." Only the words needed to reach that threshold are included in the "lottery" for the next word. The "P" can have a value between 0 and 1. A simple example: We'll use the same words as above. Let's say Top-P is 0.8 (80%). 1. "tree" (score 0.5), 2. "pole" (score 0.2). Together, this is 0.5 + 0.2 = 0.7. That's not 0.8 yet. 3. "curtains" (score 0.1). Now the sum is 0.5 + 0.2 + 0.1 = 0.8. We've reached the threshold. So, the AI will now only choose from "tree," "pole," or "curtains." The word "car" is no longer in the running, even though it was in the top 5. The clever thing about Top-P is that the number of words to choose from can change. If one word is super likely (e.g., score 0.95 and P=0.9), perhaps only that one word will be chosen. If many words are somewhat likely, the group to choose from can be larger.

These dials, Top-K and Top-P, help to channel the creativity you get from a higher temperature. They prevent the AI from choosing too many nonsensical, highly improbable words. It's like setting up a safety net. You can often experiment to see which of the two, or a combination, works best for what you want to achieve.

All the Dials Together

Now it gets really interesting: all these dials–output length, temperature, Top-K, and Top-P–work together as a team. The setting of one dial can influence how the others work. It's important to understand how they affect each other so you can configure the AI perfectly.

Here are a few examples of how they work together:

- **If you set the temperature to 0** (super well-behaved and predictable), then Top-K and Top-P don't really matter much anymore. The AI is already going to pick the most likely word, so filtering other words has little effect.
- **If you set Top-K to 1**, then temperature and Top-P also become less important. There's only one word to choose from (the most likely one), so the other settings have nothing to apply to.

- **If you set Top-P very low (close to 0)**, the AI will only choose the most likely word, making temperature and Top-K less influential again.
- **If temperature, Top-K, and Top-P are all available**, the following happens: first, the words that meet both the Top-K and Top-P criteria are selected. Then, a choice is made from *that* group of words, with the temperature determining how random that choice is..

Choosing the right combination of these settings is truly an art in itself and depends entirely on what you want to achieve with your prompt and which AI you're using. There's no magic formula that always works.

However, to give you a starting point, here is some general advice:

- **For fairly normal, coherent answers that can still be a bit creative**: try starting with a temperature of about 0.2, a Top-P of 0.95, and a Top-K of 30.
- **If you want extra creative and surprising answers**: start with a temperature of 0.9, a Top-P of 0.99, and a Top-K of 40.
- **If you want very factual, less creative answers**: try a temperature of 0.1, a Top-P of 0.9, and a Top-K of 20.
- **And if your task always has only one correct answer (like a simple math problem)**: Set the temperature to 0.

Remember: the more freedom you give the AI (higher temperature, higher Top-K, higher Top-P, and more allowed output tokens), the greater the chance that the AI will generate text that might be less relevant to your original question. It's always a search for the right balance. The most important thing is to experiment.

Try out different settings and see what works best for your specific goals. That's a core part of prompt engineering: not only is the text of the prompt important, but also how you set the "dials" of the AI.

In most cases, you won't see all these dials, but there are still plenty of AIs where you can. Top-K is often no longer an adjustable setting, but through platforms like Google AI Studio (aistudio.google.com) or the OpenAI playground (platform.openai.com/playground), you can still adjust the other dials (temperature, Top-P, and the number of allowed output tokens).

3. Prompting Techniques

Now we know what prompts are and how to adjust the AI's "dials" a bit. It's time to dive into the different ways we can create prompts. Just as there are different ways to ask a person a question, there are also various techniques for giving instructions to an AI. These techniques help the AI understand you better and provide more relevant and accurate answers.

Simple Prompting

The simplest way to talk to an AI is to just ask it a question or give it a command, without any extra frills. We call this **"General Prompting"** or, with a fancier term, **"Zero-Shot Prompting."** "Zero-shot" literally means you give the AI zero examples of what the answer should look like (the Format part of the RAFT method). You only provide a description of the task and maybe some text to start with.

For instance, you want the AI to classify a recipe as 'vegetarian,' 'vegan,' 'meat dish,' or 'fish dish' (Table 2). With a zero-shot prompt like this, it's important to keep the **temperature low**, because you don't need creativity, but rather an answer that is as objective as possible. Sometimes this simple approach works perfectly, especially if the task isn't too complicated. The AI has been trained on a massive amount of text and can often understand simple commands.

But what if the task gets trickier? Or if you want the answer to have a very specific format? Then zero-shot prompting is often not enough. The AI might misunderstand you or give an answer that isn't quite what you were looking for. Luckily, there are other techniques for that.

What?	How?
Goal	State if a recipe is 'VEGETARIAN,' 'VEGAN,' 'MEAT DISH,' or 'FISH DISH.'
Model	Language Model or LLM (e.g., ChatGPT)
Temp	0.1
Top-P	1
Token Limit	5
Prompt	State if a recipe is 'VEGETARIAN,' 'VEGAN,' 'MEAT DISH,' or 'FISH DISH.' Recipe: "Ingredients: chicken breast, bell pepper, onion, rice, soy sauce." Dish Type:
Expected Answer	MEAT DISH

Table 2: Example of a zero-shot prompt.

Providing Examples in the Prompt

If a zero-shot prompt (without examples) doesn't give you the desired result, there's a great trick: show the AI how it's done. You simply give the AI one or more examples of what you mean. We call this **"One-Shot Prompting"** (if you give one example) or **"Few-Shot Prompting"** (if you give a few examples).

Why does this work so well? AIs are very good at recognizing patterns. When you show them a few examples of the input you're giving and the output you expect, the AI often "gets" what you mean much better. It's like saying, "Look, this is how you do it!" This is especially useful when you want the answer to have a certain structure or format.

- **One-Shot Prompting**: You provide one example. The AI tries to replicate this example for your new question.

- **Few-Shot Prompting**: You provide several examples. This helps the AI see and follow the pattern even better. How many examples you need depends on how complex the task is and how smart the AI is. Usually, three to five examples are a good start.

Let's look at an example where we teach the AI to classify the emotion of sentences using emojis, so the AI adds the correct emoji(s) to a new sentence (Table 3).

What?	How?
Goal	Classify the emotion of a sentence with appropriate emojis.
Model	Language Model or LLM (e.g., ChatGPT)
Temp	0.1
Top-P	1
Token Limit	50
Prompt	Classify the following sentences with appropriate emojis: EXAMPLE: "I'm so happy about this news!" EMOTION: "Joy 😄🥳" EXAMPLE: "This is really disappointing." EMOTION: "Disappointment 😞😔" EXAMPLE: "The sun is shining and the birds are singing." EMOTION: "Positive ☀️🐦" SENTENCE: "I'm feeling a bit down today." EMOTION:
Expected Answer	"Sadness 🌧️😢"

Table 3: Example of a few-shot prompt.

Do you see how the examples help the AI? They show exactly how the input (the sentence) should be converted into the desired output (the emotion including specific emojis). The AI learns not only which emotion belongs to which sentence but also how to express that emotion with the right emojis. When choosing examples, it's important to consider:

- **Quality over quantity**: Make sure your examples are very clear, correct, and well-written. A single small mistake in an example can confuse the AI and lead to strange answers.
- **Relevance**: The examples must genuinely resemble the task you want the AI to perform.
- **Variation and "edge cases"**: If you want the AI to handle all sorts of different inputs well, provide varied examples. Also, think about "edge cases": these are unusual or unexpected inputs that the AI should still be able to process correctly. An example of an edge case could be

seen in Table 2, where the ingredients included meat as well as vegetables.

Providing good examples is one of the most important techniques in prompt engineering. It's like giving the AI a mini-training session specifically for your task. It shows the AI not only what to do but also how to think to arrive at the correct answer.

Providing Context

Sometimes you don't just want the AI to perform a task; you also want to guide *how* it performs that task, or from what perspective. For this, there are three techniques that are somewhat similar but each with a slightly different emphasis: **System Prompting**, **Contextual Prompting**, and **Role Prompting**. You'll often use them interchangeably.

- **System Prompt**: With a system prompt, you give the AI a general instruction or an overarching goal for how it should operate. You're telling it the "big picture." The name says it all: you give the "system" (the AI) an extra task or guideline. This is useful when you want the output to meet specific requirements. For example, you can instruct the AI to always provide answers in all caps (as in Table 4, where a recipe classification must be in uppercase).

- **Role Prompt**: With this prompt (the R in the RAFT method), you ask the AI to take on a specific role or persona. This helps the AI create answers that fit the knowledge, tone, and style of that role. It often makes the output more relevant and informative. You can ask the AI to take on the role of an editor giving feedback on a text, a marketing expert giving advice on product promotion, or a history teacher creating a lesson on World War II. Table 5 shows an example of a role prompt based on the history teacher.

- **Contextual Prompt**: Here, you give the AI specific details or background information relevant to the question or task. This helps the AI better understand the nuances and tailor its answer accordingly. It's like saying, "Keep this in mind when you answer." This type of prompt is very dynamic and situation-specific. It ensures the AI understands what you mean more quickly, leading to better and more relevant answers. Table 6 shows an example of a contextual prompt for a travel blog.

These three techniques –system, role, and context– help you to guide the AI much more precisely. They are not just about *what* the AI should do, but also *how*, in what *style*, and with what *background knowledge*. This is an important step in transforming a general-purpose answering machine into a useful, adaptable assistant. It allows you, the user, to truly "shape" the AI to your needs, making the results much more powerful.

What?	How?
Goal	State if a recipe is 'vegetarian,' 'vegan,' 'meat dish,' or 'fish dish.'
Model	Language Model or LLM (e.g., ChatGPT)
Temp	1
Top-P	1
Tokenlimiet	10
Prompt	Classify recipes as vegetarian, vegan, meat dish, or fish dish. Respond only in uppercase letters. Recipe: "Ingredients: lentils, spinach, coconut milk, curry paste." Dish Type:
Expected Answer	VEGAN

Table 4: Example of a system prompt.

What?	How?
Goal	Role-play as a history teacher and suggest two topics for a lesson plan on WWII.
Model	Language Model or LLM (e.g., ChatGPT, Gemini, Copilot, Claude, etc.)
Temp	1
Top-P	0.8
Token Limit	1024
Prompt	I want you to act as a history teacher. Suggest two interesting topics about World War II, and provide a brief description. Lesson Topics:
Expected Answer	1. The Rise of Totalitarian Regimes: In this lesson, we will look at how Nazism in Germany and Fascism in Italy emerged. 2. Daily Life During Occupation and Resistance: Here, we focus on the impact of the war on ordinary citizens. What was life like under occupation?

Table 5: Example of a role prompt.

What?	How?
Goal	Create a blog post about travel.
Model	Language Model or LLM (e.g., ChatGPT, Gemini, Copilot, Claude, etc.)
Temp	1
Top-P	0.8
Token Limit	1024
Prompt	Context: You are writing for a travel blog about unique, affordable city trips in Europe for young travelers. Suggest 2 blog topics with a short description.
Expected Answer	1. "Austrian Gems: Linz & Graz". This blog explores two lesser-known but vibrant cities in Austria that have a lot to offer young, budget-conscious travelers. 2. "The Cultural Hotspots: Budapest & Krakow". This blog covers the rich history and lively contemporary culture of these affordable cities, perfect for a weekend trip.

Table 6: Example of a contextual prompt.

Taking a Step Back

Sometimes you're faced with a complex question or a difficult problem, and if you ask the AI for the solution directly, you might not get the best answer. The AI might get bogged down in details or provide a superficial response. A clever technique that can help is **"Step-back Prompting."**

The idea is simple: instead of immediately asking the specific, difficult question, you first have the AI "take a step back." You ask it to think about a more general question, a higher-level concept, or the underlying principles related to the problem. You then use the answer to that general question (the "step-back" question) as extra information when you ask the AI the original, specific question again.

Imagine the AI has a super-brain, just like you. Before you solve a tough math problem, you might first think carefully about what is being asked. You try to see the big picture. That's exactly what the AI does here. By first looking from a distance and thinking about the entire problem, the AI knows better what information is important. It's as if you're helping the AI find the right knowledge in its 'memory drawers' before it starts with the details.

This way, the AI can provide much better and smarter answers. It doesn't look at small pieces right away but understands the problem as a whole. The AI is essentially doing what we do: taking a step back, looking at the problem differently, or thinking about the main ideas. Let's apply this to writing an exciting children's book. In Table 7, we'll look at the original question; in Table 8, we'll do the step-back phase; and in Table 9, we'll use the original question combined with the context (from the step-back phase).

What?	How?
Goal	Write a paragraph for a plot of an exciting children's book.
Model	Language Model or LLM (e.g., ChatGPT, Gemini, Copilot, Claude, etc.)
Temp	0.7
Top-P	0.9
Token Limit	50
Prompt	Write a plot paragraph for an exciting children's book for kids aged 8-10.
Expected Answer	A group of friends discovers a secret map that leads to a hidden treasure in the woods. They must work together to solve riddles and overcome obstacles before a mean treasure hunter beats them to it.

Table 7: Example of the original question.

What?	How?
Doel	Generate 3-5 important elements that make a children's book exciting.
Model	Language Model or LLM (e.g., ChatGPT, Gemini, Copilot, Claude, etc.)
Temp	0.5
Top-P	0.8
Token Limit	100
Prompt	Based on popular exciting children's books for ages 8-10, what are 3-5 important elements that contribute to a compelling plot?
Expected Answer	1. A mystery that needs to be solved. 2. Unexpected discoveries or secret places. 3. Friends who have to help each other and work together. 4. A mild, but clear, antagonist or challenge. 5. A touch of magic or fantasy.

Table 8: Example of the step-back phase.

What?	How?
Goal	Write a paragraph for an exciting children's book plot, based on previously generated elements.
Model	Language Model or LLM (e.g., ChatGPT, Gemini, Copilot, Claude, etc.)
Temp	0.7
Top-P	0.9
Token Limit	1024
Prompt	Context: Important elements for an exciting children's book are: a mystery; unexpected discoveries; friends working together; a touch of fantasy Now, write a paragraph for a story idea for an exciting children's book for kids aged 8-10, incorporating these elements.
Expected Answer	Luna and her little brother Max find an old, dusty telescope in the attic that leads them to a hidden star map–the mystery begins! The map points the way to a forgotten part of their city park where strange, glowing mushrooms grow–an unexpected discovery. Together with their brave dog, Puk, they must solve the riddles of the

What?	How?
	lights, while the grumpy park keeper, who doesn't want strangers in his part of the park, is hot on their heels. They discover that the mushrooms are the source of magic that can save the city, and they must work together to protect the magic.

Table 9: Asking the original question again with context.

Step-back prompting is a smart way to help the AI "dig deeper" and better utilize its knowledge, especially for more difficult tasks that require creativity or deeper insight. You are essentially guiding the AI in its thought process, which is a more intelligent way of prompting.

Chain of Thought

Sometimes you encounter problems where you can't just give the answer in one go. Think of a tricky math problem, a logical puzzle, or a question where you need to combine multiple pieces of information. For these kinds of tasks, there's a very clever technique called **"Chain of Thought Prompting" (CoT)**.

The idea is that you don't just ask the AI for the final answer, but you also task it with showing its thought process–the intermediate reasoning steps it takes to arrive at the solution. It's like in school, where for a math problem you can't just write down the answer but also have to show your work. By asking the AI to "think out loud" and create these thought steps, you often help it arrive at a better answer, especially for tasks that require reasoning. In Table 10, you can see how the AI gives a wrong answer to a difficult puzzle.

What?	How?
Goal	Solve a difficult puzzle.
Model	Language Model or LLM (e.g., ChatGPT, Gemini, Copilot, Claude, etc.)
Temp	0.1
Top-P	1
Token Limit	50
Prompt	The red car arrived earlier than the blue car, but later than the green one. The yellow car arrived last. Which car arrived second?
Expected Answer	The blue car. (This answer is incorrect).

Table 10: Example without Chain of Thought.

An easy way to turn on Chain of Thought is by adding the phrase "**Let's think step by step.**" to your prompt. You can see an example of this in Table 11.

What?	How?
Goal	Solve a difficult puzzle by using thought steps.
Model	Language Model or LLM (e.g., ChatGPT)
Temp	0.1
Top-P	1
Token Limit	150
Prompt	The red car arrived earlier than the blue one, but later than the green one. The yellow car came in last. Which car arrived second? Let's think step by step.
Expected Answer	Okay, the red car came after the green one: Green -> Red. The red car came before the blue one: Red -> Blue. The yellow car came in last. So the order is: Green, Red, Blue, Yellow. The car that arrived second is Red.

Table 11: Example of a zero-shot Chain of Thought prompt.

What?	How?
Goal	Solve a difficult puzzle using thought steps and an example.
Model	Language Model or LLM (e.g., ChatGPT)
Temp	0.1
Top-P	1
Token Limit	300
Prompt	Example Question: John lives on the third floor. Peter lives two floors below John. Linda lives one floor above Peter. Which floor does Linda live on? Example Answer: Let's determine the floors: 1. John lives on the 3rd floor. 2. Peter lives two floors below John, so on 3 - 2 = the 1st floor. 3. Linda lives one floor above Peter, so on 1 + 1 = the 2nd floor. The answer is Linda lives on the 2nd floor. New Question: The red car arrived earlier than the blue car, but later than the green one. The yellow car arrived last. Which car arrived second?

What?	How?
	Think step by step. New Answer:
Expected Answer	Let's determine the order: 1. The red car (R) arrived earlier than the blue one (B). Thus: R B. 2. The red car (R) arrived later than the green one (G). Thus: G R. 3. The yellow car (Y) came in last. Let's combine this: G R B. And Y is last. The order is therefore: Green, Red, Blue, Yellow. The car that arrived second is the Red car.

Table 12: Example of a few-shot Chain of Thought prompt.

Chain of Thought gets even better when you combine it with a few-shot prompt. You not only instruct it to think step-by-step, but you also provide one or more examples of what such a step-by-step reasoning looks like. You can see an example of this in Table 12.

- **Advantages of Chain of Thought**: It's relatively easy to apply and often works well without needing to specially train the AI. It also gives you insight into the AI's reasoning steps. If a mistake is made, you can often see where it went wrong. This opens up the AI's "black box" a little.
- **Disadvantage of Chain of Thought**: The AI's response includes the entire thought chain, so the output is longer. This costs more tokens, and therefore more time and money.

For many AI tools, Chain of Thought prompting has become a technique that is less necessary, as you can often choose an AI that does this for you automatically. Still, it can be useful to apply Chain of Thought prompting manually, especially if you notice the AI getting stuck on difficult questions or if the answers aren't precise enough. It's a handy skill to master for when you really want to go in-depth with your prompts.

Self-Consistency

Although Chain of Thought helps the AI reason better, it's not always perfect. Sometimes, if you ask the same question multiple times (especially with the "temperature dial" turned up a bit for more variation), the AI might come up with different reasoning paths and thus different answers. So which answer is the right one? For this, there's a clever technique called **"Self-Consistency."**

The idea behind self-consistency is quite logical: suppose you have a difficult problem, and you ask multiple experts for a solution. If most experts come up with the same answer (even if they used different methods to get there), you have more confidence in that answer. Self-consistency does something similar with an AI:

- **Step 1**: You take your prompt (often a Chain of Thought prompt).

- **Step 2**: You have the AI answer this prompt multiple times. By setting the temperature slightly higher, for example, you encourage the AI to explore different "thought paths."
- **Step 3**: You extract the final conclusion from each generated response.
- **Step 4**: You see which answer appears most often ("the majority rules"). That answer is then considered the most reliable one.

This improves the accuracy and consistency of the answers because it doesn't depend on a single response. Table 13 shows an example of classifying customer feedback. The feedback can be POSITIVE, NEGATIVE, or NEUTRAL. But the message is so subtle that it can be interpreted in different ways.

Attempt	AI Reasoning	Conclusion
1	Starts with "runs stable" (positive) and ends with "looks sleek" (positive). The wish for more features is a suggestion, not a strong complaint. Overall positive.	POSITIVE
2	There is a missed expectation ("was hoping for a bit more"). Although there are positive points, the dissatisfaction with the features weighs heavily. It's not fully positive or negative.	NEUTRAL
3	Stability and appearance are good, but the absence of expected features is a crucial drawback. This points to dissatisfaction with the substantive improvement. So, more on the negative side.	NEGATIVE
4	There are positive aspects ("stable," "sleek"), but also a clear point of criticism ("hoped for a few more new features"). This balances the positive and negative points, leading to a balanced opinion.	NEUTRAL

Attempt	AI Reasoning	Conclusion
5	Focus on the functional desire ("more new features"). Stability and appearance are basic expectations, while the features determine the real added value. This is a point of disappointment.	NEUTRAL

Table 13: Example of a self-consistency prompt.

Suppose you use a zero-shot Chain of Thought prompt for a tricky classification: "Classify the following customer feedback message as POSITIVE, NEGATIVE, or NEUTRAL. Think step by step and explain your reasoning."

A customer might have given this feedback: "The new update runs stable, but I was hoping for a few more new features. It does look sleek, though."

If we look at the five attempts in Table 13, we see that the conclusions vary: POSITIVE (1x), NEGATIVE (1x), and NEUTRAL (3x). According to the principle of self-consistency, we would then choose 'NEUTRAL' as the most reliable answer, because it occurred most often.

This technique is especially useful for tasks where a fixed answer is possible, such as mathematics or classifications with ambiguous meaning. The downside is that it requires more computing power and time because you have to run the same prompt multiple times. But for really tough problems where accuracy is crucial, it can be a very handy technique.

Tree of Thoughts

We've seen how Chain of Thought helps the AI think in a linear sequence of steps. Self-consistency builds on that. But what if the problem is so complex that there isn't one straight path to the solution, but multiple possible branches and choices? That's where **"Tree of Thoughts"** (ToT) comes in.

Tree of Thoughts is an even more advanced technique. Instead of having the AI follow just one thought path at a time, Tree of Thoughts allows the AI to explore multiple different reasoning paths simultaneously, just like the branches of a tree.

Imagine trying to solve a complex maze. With a zero-shot prompt, you might just walk down a random path. With Chain of Thought, you follow one specific path, step by step. If it's a dead end, you're out of luck. With Tree of Thoughts, it's like sending multiple scouts down different corridors of the maze at the same time. Each scout reports back on how promising their path seems. The AI can then decide to explore the most promising paths further and even backtrack if a path clearly leads nowhere.

The core of Tree of Thoughts is that the AI not only generates thoughts but also evaluates them. There are often two types of prompts used for this:

- **Propose Prompt**: This prompt generates possible next steps or partial solutions (the "branches" of the tree).
- **Value Prompt**: This prompt evaluates the generated steps and helps the AI decide which branches are the most promising to explore further.

Tree of Thoughts allows the AI to think more "strategically" and "goal-oriented," similar to how humans do when they have to weigh different options and plan ahead. This prompt is very costly in terms of time and computing power, as many prompts need to be generated and evaluated. Therefore, it's typically used for problems that cannot be solved well with simpler techniques like Chain of Thought.

ReAct

So far, we've mainly looked at how we can get the AI to think to arrive at an answer. But what if the AI needs information it doesn't have in its training data? Or what if it needs to perform a calculation it can't do well? That's where the **ReAct (Reason & Act)** technique comes in handy.

ReAct is super smart because it enables the AI not only to **Reason** but also to take **Actions** to gather more information or use other tools. This could include searching for information on the internet, using a calculator, or calling a piece of computer code.

It works in a cycle, a kind of loop of reason-act-observe-reason:

- **Reason**: The AI analyzes the problem and comes up with a plan. It figures out what information it's missing or what action it needs to take.

- **Act**: The AI performs the planned action. This could be a search query on a search engine, for example.
- **Observe**: The AI looks at the result of its action (e.g., the search results).
- **Reason**: Based on the new information (the observation), the AI adjusts its reasoning and makes a plan for the next step.

The AI repeats this until it has enough information to solve the problem and give a final answer. It mimics how we humans often solve problems: we think, do something to learn more, see what happens, and then think again.

In Table 14, you can see an example of ReAct. Imagine the AI needs to find out how many dogs there are in total on a whole street. You could ask this question: "How many dogs do the residents of Emma Square have?"

Step	Reasoning	Act	Observation
1	"I need to know who lives on Emma Square."	Searches via a map or program for houses on Emma Square.	Found: 5 houses on the street.
2	"Now I need to know how many dogs they have at house number 2."	Searches "number of dogs house number 2 Emma Square."	Found: two dogs.
3	"1 of 5 houses has 2 dogs. Now for house number 4."	Searches "number of dogs house number 4 Emma Square."	Found: one dog.
4	"2 of 5 houses done. Now for house number 6."	Searches "number of dogs house number 6 Emma Square."	Found: zero dogs.
5	"3 of 5 houses done. Now for house number 8."	Searches "number of dogs house number 8 Emma Square."	Found: three dogs.
6	"4 of 5 houses done. Now for house number 10."	Searches "number of dogs house number 10 Emma Square."	Found: one dog.

Step	Reasoning	Act	Observation
7	"All houses checked. Total is 2 + 1 + 0 + 3 + 1 = 7 dogs."	No further action needed.	Answer: 7 dogs.

Table 14: Example of ReAct.

ReAct is a significant step towards creating **AI agents**–systems that can perform entire tasks in complex situations without someone constantly telling them what to do. The beauty of ReAct is that it helps the AI do more than just use its learned knowledge. Normally, they can only talk about what they already know. But with ReAct, AIs can use external tools. This transforms an AI that used to just "talk like a book" into a "thinking doer." It shows how we can vastly expand the capabilities of AI by letting them ask for "outside help."

Letting the AI Create Prompts Itself

We've now seen quite a few techniques for creating better prompts ourselves. But what if writing that perfect prompt is very complicated, or if you need many different variations of a prompt? Wouldn't it be handy if the AI could help you with that? That's exactly what **Automatic Prompt Engineering (APE)** does.

With APE, you use an AI to create prompts. It's like writing a prompt to have prompts written. This can help speed up the process of creating your prompts and can even lead to better prompts than you could have come up with yourself. It works something like this:

- **Give the AI an instruction**: You tell the AI (let's call it the "prompt-generator AI") that it needs to create a number of sample prompts for a specific task.

- **Let the AI generate prompts**: The prompt-generator AI gets to work and comes up with a list full of different prompts.
- **Select the best prompts**: Then, you review the prompts the AI has generated. You pick the best ones. Maybe you tweak them a bit to make them even better. You can repeat this as many times as you like.

Imagine you want to train an AI to help children with their homework about animals. The AI needs to recognize animals when it gets a question. You also want the AI to recognize different ways children might ask this: "Is this a mammal?" The instruction to the AI could be: "We want to create a homework assistant for kids. To teach the AI, we need different ways a child might ask: 'Is this a mammal?' Come up with 10 different ways a child could ask this." The prompt-generator AI might then respond with sentences like, "Does this animal belong to the mammals?", "Does this animal have warm blood and give live birth?", "Is this critter considered a mammal?", etc.

APE is a super-skill. You're using the power of AI (their ability to generate text and see smart patterns) to make working with AI itself even better. It can save a lot of time, especially if you need many different questions for, say, training an AI or testing an AI system. Of course, you don't have to stop thinking for yourself entirely; it's still important that you check the generated prompts and choose the best ones. But it's a smart way to put the AI to work for you to make the process of creating prompts faster and better.

4. Coding Assistant

Did you know that AI isn't just good at understanding and writing human language, but also at working with computer language, also known as code? You can use an AI as a kind of personal programming assistant. This can be a huge help, whether you're a seasoned developer, just starting to code, or don't want to write any code yourself but still want to create a website or app. Let's look at a few ways you can use AI for coding.

Letting the AI Write Code

One of the most obvious applications is asking the AI to write code for you. Imagine you have a tedious job, like converting photos to a smaller format. You might know this can be done with a script (a small computer program), but writing that script takes time, especially if you haven't mastered the programming language.

Instead, you can give the AI a prompt, and the computer can automatically create a website that converts and optimizes your images (as shown in Table 15).

The AI can then produce a complete script, often even with comments included to explain what the code does. This can save you a tremendous amount of time.

Important: Even though AI can often generate impressive code, you must always read, understand, and, most importantly, test the code yourself before using it. AI can make mistakes or create code that doesn't do exactly what you expect, or that might even be insecure.

What?	How?
Goal	Convert and optimize images to .webp
Model	Language Model or LLM (e.g., ChatGPT, Gemini, Copilot, Claude, etc.)
Temp	0.1
Top-P	1
Token Limit	1024
Prompt	Write a piece of code in a single HTML file. This file must be able to convert images like .jpg and .png to .webp. The file size must be optimized, but the image quality should be preserved.
Expected Answer	A single HTML file with code like this (https://thefuture.im/prompts/webp)

Table 15: Example of writing code.

Now, the most fun part is to test this. We can use the code already generated in Table 15.

Follow these steps:

- **Download the answer from Table 15**: Go to the website thefuture.im/prompts/webp and copy the code.
- **Paste the code**: Paste the code into a text editor (like Notepad or TextEdit) and save it as image.html.
- **Convert your image:** Open the image.html file in your browser and click the "Choose Image" button. Select the image you want to convert. Then, click the "Convert" button. You will automatically get an optimized image that has been converted to a .webp file.

Letting the AI Explain Code

Do you work in a team, or are you looking at code you wrote a long time ago? Sometimes it can be quite difficult to understand exactly what a piece of code does. Here, too, the AI can be a lifesaver. You can give the AI a piece of code and ask it to explain it in plain English.

What?	How?
Goal	Have the code explained.
Model	Language Model or LLM (e.g., ChatGPT, Gemini, Copilot, Claude, etc.)
Temp	0.1
Top-P	1
Tokenlimiet	1024
Prompt	Explain in simple language what the main purpose of this code is. Don't give details: [INSERT THE CODE FROM THEFUTURE.IM/PROMPTS/WEBP HERE].
Expected Answer	It's a webpage that allows you to convert JPG and PNG images to the modern WebP format and then easily download them.

Table 16: Example of having code explained.

Table 16 shows an explanation of the code without going into detail. But you can also have the AI describe what each line or block of code does, step by step. This is super handy for quickly understanding how unfamiliar code works and for testing your own coding knowledge.

Letting the AI Translate Code

Suppose you have a piece of code in one programming language (like HTML), but you actually need it in another language (like Swift, because you want to build a mobile app with it). Instead of rewriting everything manually, you can ask the AI to translate the code for you (see Table 17).

The AI will then try to write equivalent code that has the same functionality. The same rule applies here: always review and test the translated code thoroughly. The translation may not always be 100% perfect, but it can be a great starting point.

What?	How?
Goal	Translate HTML code to Swift code.
Model	Language Model or LLM (e.g., ChatGPT, Gemini, Copilot, Claude, etc.)
Temp	0.1
Top-P	1
Token Limit	1024
Prompt	Translate this HTML code [INSERT THE CODE FROM THEFUTURE.IM/PROMPTS/WEBP HERE] to Swift. The Swift code must create a mobile app with the same functionality.
Expected Answer	A single Swift file with code like this: (https://thefuture.im/prompts/swift)

Table 17: Example of having code translated.

Letting AI Find Errors in Code

Every programmer makes mistakes (bugs). Finding those mistakes (debugging) can sometimes be frustrating and time-consuming. But here, too, your AI buddy can help.

What?	How?
Goal	Add two numbers in Python (2 + 3 = 5).
Broken Code	num1 = input("First number: ") num2 = input("Second number: ") result = num1 + num2 print("Sum:", result)
Expected Answer	23

Table 18: Example of broken Python code.

Table 18 shows an example of broken Python code. You want the code to add 2 + 3. You should get the answer 5, but this code gives you 23. You can solve this problem with AI (as in Table 19).

What?	How?
Doel	Fixing the bug in the Python code.
Model	Language Model or LLM (e.g., ChatGPT)
Temp	0.1
Top-P	1
Token Limit	1024
Prompt	I'm using this Python code and getting an error: num1 = input("First number: ") num2 = input("Second number: ") result = num1 + num2 print("Sum:", result) The code concatenates the numbers instead of adding them. Explain what's wrong in one sentence and correct the code.
Expected Answer	What's wrong is that input() treats the input as text, causing the numbers to be stuck together instead of being added. num1 = float(input("First number: ")) num2 = float(input("Second number: ")) result = num1 + num2 print("Sum:", result)

Table 19: Corrected Python code with a explanation.

In Table 19, things go right. You not only get a short explanation of the problem but also the solution to the error right away.

These kinds of code prompts are not just a huge productivity booster for experienced developers; they can also be a great learning tool for beginners. The AI can act as a patient mentor who helps you improve your code and teaches you new things. It lowers the barrier to entry and can speed up the learning process.

5. What else?

We've already looked at a whole range of ways we can talk to AI using text prompts. It sometimes feels like the possibilities are endless, from generating text to answering difficult questions. But development isn't standing still; in fact, it's accelerating. So, let's take a quick peek at what else is possible. We'll explore the latest innovations and look ahead to what the future might bring us in the world of AI.

Pictures, Videos, and Sound

So far, we've mostly talked about prompts that consist of text you type. But imagine if you could give the AI not just text, but also a picture, an audio clip, or even a video as part of your prompt. That's exactly what **"Multimodal Prompting"** is. "Multi" means "more," and "modal" refers to the "mode" or "form" of input. So, multiple forms of input at the same time.

Instead of just typing, "Write a poem about a sunset on the beach," with multimodal prompting, you could upload a beautiful photo of a sunset and add the text prompt, "Write a poem inspired by this image." Or you could provide an audio clip of birdsong and ask, "What bird species do I hear in this audio clip, and describe its characteristics?"

Why is this so exciting? The world around us isn't just made of text. We humans communicate and experience the world through all our senses: we see, hear, and feel. To make AI truly intelligent and useful in all sorts of situations, they also need to understand information that isn't text. AIs that can handle multiple types of input–"multimodal models"–can therefore often create better answers. They can make connections between, for example, an image and a text, or sound and a video.

This is a significant step toward AI that understands the world better, more like we humans do. It opens the door to completely new ways of communicating with AI. It will make AI even smarter and ensure that we encounter it more and more in our daily lives.

6. My Golden Rules

We have now discussed a whole range of techniques that can help you talk effectively with AI. To help you become a true master—and thus get the most out of your conversations—I want to share my "golden rules" with you. These are the best tips and tricks ("best practices," as they're called) that I've gathered over the years. If you follow these, you'll find that your prompts will steadily improve, and the AI's results will be much more accurate and relevant.

Rule 1: Provide Examples

This is perhaps the most important rule of all. Just like when you're teaching a child to ride a bike, it helps immensely if you show them how a few times first. So, give the AI examples (one-shot or few-shot) of exactly what you want. The AI learns from these examples and can then perform your specific task much better. It's like giving the AI a small, customized lesson.

Rule 2: Keep It Simple

Use clear, simple words in your prompts. Try to avoid complicated sentences and unnecessary information. A good rule of thumb is: if you find the prompt complicated to read, the AI will probably find it even harder to understand.

Also, try to use active verbs that clearly describe the action. Think of words like: analyze, describe, create, classify, define, evaluate, generate, identify, make, organize, select, sort, summarize, translate, find, write. Here are examples of a bad and a good prompt:

- **Bad**: "Given the fact that I currently reside in the metropolis of New York, I would be pleased to be informed about excellent locations suitable for a visit, also in light of the presence of my two three-year-old children, in order to optimize our vacation."
- **Good**: "Act as a tour guide for tourists. Describe fun places to visit in Manhattan, New York with a 3-year-old child."

Rule 3: State What You Want to Get

Don't just say "write a story," but be as specific as possible. The clearer you are about the desired result, the better the AI can help you.

- **Bad**: "Generate a blog post about game consoles."
- **Good:** "Create a 3-paragraph blog post about the top 5 game consoles. The blog post should be informative and engaging, written in a conversational style."

Rule 4: Focus on What to Do

It's often better to tell the AI what it *should* do, rather than listing all the things it *shouldn't* do. Positive instructions are clearer and give the AI more direction.

- **Bad:** "Generate a paragraph about the top 5 game consoles. Don't mention any game names."

- **Good:** "Create a paragraph about the top 5 game consoles. Discuss only the console, the company that made it, the year it was released, and its total sales figures."

Of course, there are times when you do need to say what's not allowed, for example, to prevent harmful responses, but try to give positive instructions as much as possible.

Rule 5: Pay Attention to Length

Think about how long you want the answer to be. You can set this with the token limit, but you can also ask for it in your prompt itself, like "Explain quantum physics in a message the length of a tweet."

Rule 6: Use Variables

If you want to use a prompt multiple times but with slightly different input each time, you can use **"variables."** A variable is a kind of placeholder that you can fill in later.

- **Variables**: {city} = "Amsterdam".
- **Prompt**: "You are a tour guide. Tell me a fun fact about the city: {city}."
- **Answer**: "Amsterdam is a beautiful city full of canals, bridges, and narrow streets..."

You can then change the {city} variable to "Paris" or "Rome" without having to retype the entire prompt.

Rule 7: Use Different Methods

Don't be afraid to experiment. Use different AI tools, settings, word choices, and ways of asking your question. They can all yield different results. Try phrasing your prompt as a question, a direct command, or a statement. See what works best for your goal.

Rule 8: Mix Your Examples

If you're using few-shot prompting for classification tasks (e.g., labeling something as "good" or "bad"), make sure to vary the order of your examples. Don't give three examples of "good" and then three of "bad," but mix them up. This helps the AI learn the actual characteristics of each class, rather than just memorizing the order of the examples. Start with about 6 examples and see how accurate it becomes from there.

Rule 9: Keep Learning

The world of AI is changing at lightning speed. AI tools are updated, gain new capabilities, and are trained on new information. Stay informed about these changes. Try out newer versions and adapt your prompts to take advantage of new features.

Rule 10: Use Different Response Formats

Don't just think about the question (your prompt), but also about the desired answer. Especially for tasks that aren't necessarily creative, such as those involving data, selection, sorting, or categorizing, it can be very useful to ask the AI to return the output in a structured format like JSON or XML.

Rule 11: Collaborate

If you're stuck or trying to come up with a really good prompt for a tricky problem, ask others to brainstorm with you. When multiple people, all following these golden rules, give it a try, you'll see that many different good ideas emerge.

Rule 12: Write Everything Down

Dit is misschien wel de saaiste, maar super belangrijke regel. Houd een logboek bij. Schrijf gedetailleerd op:

- **Goal**: What was the purpose of your prompt?
- **Prompt Text**: What text did you use in the prompt?
- **Model**: Which AI model did you use?
- **Settings**: What settings (temperature, Top-P, token limit) did you use?
- **Answer**: What was the response? Was the answer good or bad?
- **Improvement**: What ideas do you have for improvement?

Why is this so important? Because an AI's response can differ by model, by setting, and even by the version of the same model. Even with identical prompts, you can sometimes see slight differences in answers. By documenting everything carefully, you learn over time what works and what doesn't. You can look back, compare, and pick up your work more easily after a break. It also helps you to find errors and test the performance of your prompts on new models.

Table 20 shows a simple template for such a logbook.

Name	[name and version of your prompt]
Goal	[the sentence explaining the purpose of the prompt]
Model	[name and version of the AI model used]
Temerature	[value between 0 and 1]
Top-P	[number]
Token Limit	[number]
Prompt	[write the entire prompt here]
Answer	[write the AI's response here]

Table 20: A template for keeping track of your prompts.

These golden rules aren't just random; they have emerged from countless experiments and expert experiences. By applying them, you will move from random trial-and-error to a more methodical and effective way of prompting. Prompt engineering is a process of trying, analyzing, documenting, and refining. It's the transition from a beginner to a true pro.

7. Solving the Puzzle

Wow, what an incredible journey we've taken together through the fascinating, and sometimes dizzying, world of prompt engineering. When we started this adventure, the landscape of AI might have been an unknown and foggy territory. But now, after all these examples and techniques, I hope that the fog has lifted. The separate puzzle pieces we picked up along the way–from the simple RAFT method to advanced techniques like ReAct–now form a clear picture. Let's take one last, in-depth look at the treasure chest of knowledge you've just built, so you can confidently close this book and step into the world of AI.

What Have We Learned?

1. **Prompts Are Your Key to AI**: A prompt is your question or command to a smart large language model (LLM). The clearer and better your prompt, the better the AI's answer will be. And remember: anyone can learn to write good prompts.
2. **The RAFT Method as a Starting Point**: For beginners, the RAFT method (Role, Audience, Format, Task) is a handy mnemonic to think about your prompts in a simple way. It's a great start, but it takes more to become a pro.
3. **Prompt Engineering Is Tinkering and Puzzling**: It's the process of designing, testing, and refining your prompts until you get the desired answer. It's a skill you develop by doing.

4. **The Magic Dials of AI**: Besides the prompt text, you can often also adjust settings like output length (tokens), temperature (serious vs. creative), Top-K, and Top-P (ways to filter choices). These dials work together and strongly influence how the AI responds.
5. **Smart Prompting Tricks**: We've seen a whole host of techniques.
    - **Zero-shot**: Simply asking a question, without examples.
    - **One-Shot & Few-Shot**: Giving the AI one or more examples to learn the pattern.
    - **System, Role & Context Prompting**: Giving the AI a general task, a specific personality, or relevant background information.
    - **Step-back Prompting**: Asking a more general question first to get the AI on the right track.

- **Chain of Thought**: Asking the AI to show its thought process, which often leads to better answers for complex problems.
- **Self-Consistency (The Majority Rules)**: Asking the same question multiple times and choosing the most frequent answer to increase reliability.
- **Tree of Thoughts**: Allowing the AI to explore multiple thought paths simultaneously, like the branches of a tree.
- **ReAct (Reason & Act)**: Letting the AI think *and* take actions (like searching the internet) to gather information.
- **Automatic Prompt Engineering (APE)**: Having the AI create prompts itself to help you.

6. **Coding Assistant:** You can use AI to write, explain, translate, and even help you find errors in code.
7. **Multimodal:** Prompts will increasingly contain not only text but also pictures, sound, and video.
8. **My Golden Rules:** The 12 rules we discussed in the previous chapter, such as providing examples, keeping it simple, being specific, experimenting, and most importantly: keeping a detailed log of everything.

You Can Do This

The most important thing I want you to take away from this is that writing a prompt is something you can learn. It might seem complicated, but by practicing, experimenting, and applying the techniques and rules from this book, you too will become better and better at "talking" with AI.

The world of AI is changing fast, but the skill of creating good prompts will only become more important in the future. It ensures that you can harness the power of AI for all your goals, whether for your work, your studies, or just for fun. You are no longer at the mercy of the "magic" of AI; you have now learned how the mechanisms work and how you can influence them.

So, get started! Try out the things you've learned. Make mistakes, learn from them, and get a little better every day. I hope this book has given you a significant push in the right direction. Good luck and have fun on your own prompting adventure.

Robbert van Empel

About the Author

Robbert van Empel (b. 1984) is a Dutch AI expert and sought-after speaker who helps companies, governments, schools, and non-profits implement artificial intelligence in practical and responsible ways. After his studies at the University of Amsterdam and Leiden University, he specialized in the strategic side of AI integration: how to translate groundbreaking technology into concrete, scalable solutions.

Known for his minimalist, smartphone-free lifestyle, Van Empel focuses on sustainable innovations with maximum impact and minimal noise. He regularly appears in magazines, podcasts, and on TV shows to provide commentary on AI developments and gives keynotes throughout the country, inspiring executives and professionals with sharp analyses and practical examples.

In addition to his speaking engagements, he leads an AI research group that investigates how organizations can best implement AI into their work processes. His background in education ensures a clear, accessible narrative perspective, while his work ranges from international boardrooms to practice-oriented research projects.

When he is not speaking or writing, Robbert enjoys a balanced family life in The Netherlands with his partner and two children.

www.ingramcontent.com/pod-product-compliance
Lightning Source LLC
Chambersburg PA
CBHW050530240926
51846CB00003B/759
9789083575919